Dado Castello Branco

Timeless Brazilian
Architecture and Interiors

Timeless Brazilian Architecture and Interiors

Dado

Dado Castello Branco

Book Development by Ricardo van Steen
Text by Allex Colontonio

Rizzoli
New York
New York · Paris · London · Milan

We dedicate this book
to the clients who
believe in our work,
to our team,
the collaborators,
the supporters who made
this book possible,
and to everyone
who loves architecture
and interior design.

Table of Contents

Foreword

This third book showcasing the work of architect Dado Castello Branco offers far more than a collection of photogenic snapshots of recent projects. The pages ahead have been thoughtfully choreographed around three essential themes. First, this volume is a milestone in Dado's thirty-year professional journey. Second, it represents his first coffee table book published by Rizzoli, the renowned Italian house with a global reach, and this speaks volumes about the brand's growing international presence. While Dado continues to design projects across Brazil—a country celebrated for its diversity and vast scale, as well as being a cornerstone of Modernism—he has long been expanding his reach, with residences in Lisbon, London, Paris, Miami, New York, and Philadelphia, where he completed his first international project more than two decades ago. And third, while he is not yet planning a generational transition, he proudly introduces here the idea of continuity through his son, Guilherme, an architect who has been part of the studio for eight years and now serves as its general director.
With so much to share and few words to spare, the homes have been presented in a fluid and intuitive way, less Cartesian in nature, but guided by the principles of light, materials, the horizon, and art. These are the foundational elements that steer Dado's work, acting as a compass to create homes that speak profoundly of those who live in them and, in turn, reflect the Castello Branco ethos.

Dado Castello Branco Architecture

Born in São Paulo—the world's twenty-first largest economy, with a GDP surpassing entire countries such as Belgium, Chile, or Singapore—Dado Castello Branco celebrates three decades of a career firmly established among the leading names in contemporary Brazilian architecture. His work resonates internationally, yet without the clichés of tropical folklore: it's a cosmopolitan signature that has taken him far beyond the borders of South America.

It's no exaggeration to say that he occupies a distinctive space among his peers, embodying a contemporary vision of Neo-Modernism. Whether designing urban apartments, sprawling weekend homes in the countryside or by the sea, or even corporate and commercial spaces, his work offers a warm, humanized take on what it means to inhabit space in our day. This approach strikes a balance between the German minimalism of the Bauhaus and the classic maximalism of European traditions, whether French or British. One of his key inspirations is the American architect Philip Johnson, the first recipient of the Pritzker Prize. But perhaps Dado's work could also be placed in a subtle liminal space, bridging two giants of Modernism: Oscar Niemeyer (1907–2012), the epitome of Brazilian Modernism and master of curves, and Le Corbusier (1887–1965), the French-Swiss architect regarded as the father of the movement and champion of straight lines. Dado's projects reflect a balance between the precision of Niemeyer in the volumetric design of structures and Corbu's signature organic flow in room layouts. His designs invariably feature open floor plans with wide perspective, abundant natural light, cross ventilation, seamless spatial relationships between indoors and outdoors, and a welcoming atmosphere marked by a harmonious play of understated colors and textures.

Seamless spatial relationships between indoors and outdoors, FM Beach House

Art — one of Beatriz Milhazes's masterpieces, FAZ Residence

Horizon — view from LJT Apartment

Light — lights and shadows, FAZ Residence

Materials — details of the sofa, EA Beach House

This sensibility feels innate for a professional who graduated in Architecture and Urbanism from Centro Universitário Belas Artes de São Paulo and later studied at École Spéciale d'Architecture in Paris—a journey that mirrored Niemeyer's and Le Corbusier's encounters at pivotal points in their careers.

Guilherme Castello Branco

Guilherme Castello Branco, also a graduate of the same institution, has risen to the helm of the studio after nearly a decade of intense work alongside his father. While Dado is far from retiring, he has already laid the foundation for the brand's longevity, ensuring its originality while keeping one foot firmly planted in the future. "Guilherme started as part of our architecture team, which now includes around thirty professionals, and steadily carved out his space over the past eight years, eventually becoming general director," Dado shares. "It's a privilege when a child chooses to walk your path. In addition to Guilherme, our team is very young, which helps us stay connected to the spirit of the times."

The studio's international expansion, set to grow exponentially with the opening of a branch in Lisbon to meet the high demand for projects in Portugal, has been a long time in the making. It began early in Dado's career with works in Philadelphia, and evolved into projects in New York, Miami, Paris, and London.

From structure to substance, the studio's approach is often likened to haute couture in its comprehensive, 360-degree scope, which frequently extends to product design, including award-winning custom furniture and objects. It's about more than form and function, furniture selection, or art curation. "From the specific stitching on a sofa to the details of a handle, along with custom fabrics and rugs, we strive to create bespoke comfort and well-being, resulting in compositions deeply imbued with the owner's personality yet adaptable anywhere in the world," Guilherme explains.

Dado Castello Branco

"I've never mentioned this in an academic setting, but perhaps architecture schools should incorporate psychology as a discipline," Dado muses. "When designing for others, we engage with their intimate worlds, their deeply personal universes. Decoding their desires and expectations, and understanding the relationships they'll form within the space, is crucial. Architecture and decoration profoundly influence how people live together. Realizing how spaces change habits, lifestyles, schedules, even the way people dress, is truly fascinating. Our goal is to make our clients want to come home and stay there. To achieve that, we need to interpret them with the utmost sensitivity."

Horizon — view from
FM Beach House

Materials — details of
a handle, AS Apartment

Light — texture and mirror,
Lisbon Apartment

Art — work by Frans
Krajcberg, LJT Apartment

Experience the perfect placement of everyday objects, TF Residence

In this sense, architecture and decoration are inseparable. "They're one and the same thing. Sometimes, I start a house —or even a site plan—from the sofa. It's essential to know where someone will sit to look at that tree, contemplate the horizon, or experience the perfect ergonomics and placement of everyday objects. Some purist architects focus solely on the structure, downplaying the importance of interior spaces. For me, it's vital to be there at the beginning, middle, and end of every project."

This level of personalization in industrial design stems from both the need for site-specific solutions and the personal desire for ergonomics on a human scale. "One of our trademarks is meticulous detailing, from custom cabinetry to finish quality and harmonious compositions that often include exclusive pieces. Although I rarely have time to focus on furniture design, I take every opportunity to refine this craft," Dado concludes.

"We are uncompromising when it comes to personalization—we're extremely rigorous," Guilherme states in his role as the new face of the Castello Branco legacy. "The legacy my father has built fills me with pride. He started the studio the same year I was born. I grew up in it, witnessing every stage, every transformation, every major project, exhibition, and event. This profoundly influenced my career choice. While we share a similar perspective, I also bring other references and a strong interest in new technologies—I've implemented these innovations in the studio, where we constantly pursue the latest advancements," he adds, reflecting on the very essence of both father and son, which is revealed through the pages of this third book about the studio.

Oscar Niemeyer, Armchair, EA Apartment

Croatia
Montenegro
Brazil

The first pulse of architecture, a poetry as silent as it is radiant, luminosity is treated as more than just a compass by the studio.

Light

“Light is the guiding thread of design,” says Dado Castello Branco. The first pulse of architecture, a poetry as silent as it is radiant, luminosity is treated as more than just a compass by the studio. “When I open the door of a house, I want to see far, to capture as much sunlight as possible, without barriers, without obstacles,” he continues. In the projects that follow, whether or not the guiding lines are visible to the naked eye, the spaces are enriched by carefully harnessed natural light or lighting design solutions that aim for a performance that is more organic than theatrical, totally free of artificiality.

MLL Residence

São Paulo, Brazil
Area: 780 sqm (8,400 square feet)
Photography: Marco Antonio

The wooden facade offers a first glimpse of the project's organic character. Built from scratch in a densely wooded area of São Paulo, the residence boasts a unique feature: the pathways were landscaped by Isabel Duprat and seem to flow seamlessly into the interiors, creating a natural connection to the neighboring property, owned by the resident's brother. This thoughtful integration reflects the family's tradition of gathering daily for shared meals. A striking wall of *Monstera deliciosa*, a species native to Central America and beloved in Brazil, adds drama to the social area's lush green canvas, while a wide canopy shelters the walkway to the second house. "The expansive openings, generous wooden eaves, and 3.5-meter (11.5-foot) ceiling height amplify the feeling of spaciousness," explains Guilherme Castello Branco.

LIBRARIES
TASCHEN

HP Apartment

São Paulo, Brazil
Area: 497 sqm (5,350 square feet)
Photography: Fran Parente

Designed for a young couple with two children, this apartment in São Paulo is characterized by a double-height living room that is transformed into a veritable art gallery. A prominent painting by English artist Ian Davenport anchors the space, complemented by other vibrant works, including pieces by the Italian-born painter Alfredo Volpi. The neutral palette highlights meticulous wood paneling that transitions seamlessly into an extensive library. The furniture is a refined blend of robust Brazilian design classics and sleek Italian pieces, celebrating both comfort and craftsmanship. With a layout reminiscent of a single-story house, the apartment was custom-tailored to suit the owners' lifestyle, particularly their love of hosting guests. A well-appointed gourmet kitchen area integrates with the main living spaces, while the hallway leading to the private quarters opens up to the living room, further enhancing the sense of flow and openness.

Panelinha
1001 WHISKIES
Whisky Classified
SICILIA

O ESTADO DE S. PAULO
ELLIOTT ERWITT
REGARDING WOMEN

VIK MUNIZ
INHOTIM
PERFUME DE SONHO

DESTINATIONS
LUXURY HOTELS

TAILORING LEGENDS

APS Country House

São Paulo, Brazil
Area: 932 sqm (10,000 square feet)
Photography: Fran Parente

Nestled amid lush natural surroundings and enhanced by Gilberto Elkis's understated landscaping, this countryside estate in São Paulo's interior was originally designed by the studio two decades ago. The subtle colonial charm of its white facade and gabled roofs reflects the property's timeless elegance. The clients, a large family known for their weekend gatherings with friends, recently commissioned a major renovation that introduced contemporary volumes. A new guest house now complements the two existing buildings, while the main residence received a much-needed update. The program includes a state-of-the-art gourmet kitchen with a sprawling island, three large dining tables, and inviting seating areas. A spa, gym, and semi-Olympic pool, with stone pathways creating a visually stunning pattern from above, add to the home's appeal. The finishes are defined by glass, wood, and stone, lending the whole a natural sophistication. Set within the gardens, a charming chapel serves as a quiet testament to the family's faith.

APS Country House

AS Apartment

São Paulo, Brazil
Area: 450 sqm (4,850 square feet)
Photography: Romulo Fialdini

Once dark and compartmentalized, this apartment offered little connection to the surrounding treetops rising at its precise elevation. Dado Castello Branco orchestrated a complete transformation, tearing down walls and integrating the balcony to create fluid spaces and seamless sightlines. Spaces are elegantly defined through layout and a dramatic floor-to-ceiling brise soleil screen—a standout feature of the exceptional woodwork. Nearly rivaling the view, the apartment's powerful art collection showcases works by Julio Le Parc, Abraham Palatnik, José Patrício, Vik Muniz, and other icons of Brazilian concrete art. The furniture selection is equally curated, featuring pieces by Oscar Niemeyer, Sergio Rodrigues, and Jorge Zalszupin, alongside antique treasures such as nineteenth-century chests.

FERNAND LÉGER

R EYE IS MY MIRROR

HOTEL STORIES

YOUR EYE IS MY MIRROR

GAUGUIN
ITALIAN DREAM

PAUL KLEE
MODIGLIANI
CHANEL
JAZZ COVERS
CILDO

The foundation of each project lies in this aesthetic harmony, tactile and thermal comfort, achieved through an organic and integral approach.

Materials

Concrete, stone, metal, wood, ceramics, glass, and textiles define the architecture and interiors, shaping spaces imbued with warmth, comfort, and a tactile invitation. Regarding the materiality of their projects, Dado and Guilherme Castello Branco explain: “Unity is fundamental when combining raw materials. We prefer a restrained approach to selecting floors, walls, and facades. We appreciate the idea of continuity, as well as the authenticity of natural materials.” Far beyond structural supports, the foundation of each project lies in this aesthetic harmony, tactile and thermal comfort, achieved through an organic and integral approach. Avoiding technological homogenization, the studio takes great care in utilizing resources based on a strong commitment to environmental responsibility.

CM Residence

São Paulo, Brazil
Area: 1,200 sqm (13,000 square feet)
Photography: Douglas Friedman

From the fluid layout to the striking landscaping by Isabel Duprat and the impressive art collection, this project has so many highlights that it's hard to rank them. Yet the sculptural spiral staircase, enclosed in exquisite woodwork, undoubtedly steals the show. Serving as the backbone of the house, it anchors a spacious home where the main challenge was to fit the ambitious program into a seemingly constrained plot. "We embraced verticality, dividing the volume into four levels: basement, ground floor with social and service areas, a second floor for the bedrooms, and a top level for the spa and gym. It's an extremely contemporary house with no formal entrance. The atrium immediately reveals the sculptural staircase connecting all floors," explains Guilherme Castello Branco. Designed for a family with three children, the house seamlessly integrates with its gardens through discreet, fully embedded window frames.

domus
PICASSO

CM Residence

Lisbon Apartment

Lisbon, Portugal
Area: 220 sqm (2,370 square feet)
Photography: Filippo Bamberghi

"In this project, we had the freedom to be bolder with the palette, inspired by the owners' personalities and the richness of the local culture," says Dado Castello Branco. The interiors of the apartment, which is located in one of Europe's most vibrant capitals, come alive with warm tones, such as the mustard hue that takes center stage in the living room, paired with a painting by Christian Rosa. The rich palette is balanced by beige and gray furnishings and pronounced wooden elements that lend harmony and depth. This chromatic energy extends beyond the living space: patterned wallpapers bring texture to the bedrooms, while the kitchen features classic blue-and-white Portuguese tiles, an homage to the owners' emotional connection to local traditions. "We even sourced a set of eighteenth-century tile fragments to highlight this essence," notes the architect. Designed for a retired couple who frequently host their children and grandchildren, the apartment feels deeply personal, with their fingerprints embedded in every corner.

Lisbon Apartment

PEONIES
PORTUGAL

D. PEDRO V
MARIA FILOMENA MÓNICA
ADRIANA VAREJÃO
MAGNUM MAGNUM
MAGNUM

DRY GARDENS

FAZ Residence

São Paulo, Brazil
Area: 1,250 sqm (13,450 square feet)
Photography: Romulo Fialdini

Nestled near Ibirapuera Park—one of Latin America's largest urban green spaces—this house masterfully erases the boundaries between inside and outside: it's a true urban oasis bathed in natural light. "The entire project is oriented toward the gardens, beautifully crafted by Gilberto Elkis. We elevated the brick upper structure while enclosing the lower level with large glass panels, eliminating any physical barriers to the landscape," explains Guilherme Castello Branco. The fully open living space feels at one with the surrounding vegetation and sits just steps from the pool. Brazilian modernist classics, such as Jorge Zalszupin's furniture, coexist effortlessly with robust Italian designs and exclusive pieces by Dado Castello Branco himself, who has long contributed to product design. Walls serve as understated consoles for an impressive contemporary art collection, creating a harmonious interplay between full and empty spaces. "The mix of brick and concrete, combined with the lightness of glass, achieves a refined yet unconventional balance," concludes the architect.

FAZ Residence

TF Residence

São Paulo, Brazil
Area: 1,100 sqm (11,850 square feet)
Photography: Fran Parente

Respecting the legacy of significant architectural structures is a core principle for Dado Castello Branco. In this private residence, the studio was tasked with updating the project while introducing entirely new volumes. From the outside, the 1950s house retains its original restored facade and style, but inside, the transformation is truly dramatic. "We removed everything that couldn't be preserved, modernizing the structure while paying homage to its history. You'll see those classic touches in the ceiling moldings and baseboards," explains Guilherme Castello Branco. New additions include a spa/gym and a game room, each with its own identity. "One was designed as a wood-clad box, the other was finished in stone," he adds. Brazilian mid-century design classics by Jean Gillon and Zanine Caldas share space with iconic international labels, such as Cassina and Paola Lenti. The gardens, designed by Daniel Nunes, complement the home's graceful evolution.

ARL Residence

São Paulo, Brazil
Area: 630 sqm (6,780 square feet)
Photography: Marco Antonio

"The original house was demolished and we designed a new residence tailored to the couple's current stage in life, now that their children have moved out," says Dado Castello Branco. Built on a compact 500-square-meter (5,300-square-foot) plot, the three-story project prioritizes practicality, flow, and ease of maintenance: "We crafted a dynamic layout that reflects their lifestyle as frequent travelers." The rooftop houses the couple's suite and home office; the second floor features a cozy family room, the children's suites, and a living area with a garden view; and the lower level accommodates a gym, garage, and the husband's workshop. "We focused on delivering a well-resolved floor plan within a limited footprint, incorporating a diverse program while ensuring a harmonious connection to nature," concludes the architect. The lush vertical garden, designed by Gilberto Elkis, enhances the project's connection to its natural surroundings.

ARL Residence

KATZ

HIRST

136

The horizon emerges as a line of connection between human creation and the natural world, a threshold where dimensions converge.

Horizon

It's almost about blending with the landscape. The horizon emerges as a line of connection between human creation and the natural world, a threshold where dimensions converge. In this respect, Dado Castello Branco echoes architect Tadao Ando's philosophy: "Architecture should rise from the earth, not be imposed upon it." With minimal compartmentalization, where each structure integrates with rather than dominates the others, the studio's projects "seek perspective: we frame the landscape and aim to bring the surroundings indoors, without barriers, achieving maximum spatial integration." Thus, their architecture is not merely a capsule but an extension of the world itself.

FM Beach House

Paraty, Brazil
Area: 600 sqm (6,460 square feet)
Photography: Fernando Guerra

“Incorporating such a complete program into a limited plot was a true challenge,” remarks Dado Castello Branco about this beachside home in the Laranjeiras Condominium, in the historic town of Paraty, Rio de Janeiro. A seamless extension of its surroundings, the house blurs the boundary between the deck and the shoreline. The studio’s signature elegance shines through in the light-filled, expansive circulation spaces. “The architectural volume strikes a perfect balance of stone, wood, and glass, while the interiors feature a curated mix of Brazilian and Italian furniture, such as the armchairs by Vico Magistretti and Patricia Urquiola,” notes the architect. A sculptural, sinuous staircase leads to the upper level, enhancing the home’s architectural rhythm without yielding to excess. Rodrigo Oliveira’s landscaping reconnects the house to nature, creating an effortless dialogue between architecture and the surrounding environment.

MONTE CARLO
PALM BEACH
Lee

EA Beach House

Praia da Baleia, São Sebastião, Brazil
Area: 470 sqm (5,060 square feet)
Photography: Fran Parente

Visual permeability and perspective are intrinsic to Dado Castello Branco's projects, and this beach house is no exception. Without direct beach access or ocean views, the house embraces the lush landscaping by Daniel Nunes and the breathtaking topography of the surrounding Serra do Mar. This natural horizon served as a compass for the project's interiors: "The layout prioritizes these gardens and views, making use of expansive openings and terraces. The interiors feel like open-air balconies designed for contemplation," explains Guilherme Castello Branco. The atmosphere is casual yet elegant, defined by tactile textures, robust furniture, and chromatic accents provided by the artwork of Vik Muniz and Beatriz Milhazes. Moving beyond the traditional Caiçara aesthetics, the home invites relaxation and connects seamlessly to its surroundings.

ROMA

LJT Apartment

São Paulo, Brazil
Area: 591 sqm (6,360 square feet)
Photography: Fran Parente

With its privileged skyline views—one side overlooks the city and the other faces a vast green park—this apartment is a dynamic hub of activity. Designed for a sociable couple, passionate art collectors, and design enthusiasts, the space reflects their vibrant personalities. Their atypical request to the architects was a bar on the terrace: "The terrace has become an extension of the social area, allowing them to fully enjoy the view," explains Guilherme Castello Branco. Custom woodwork was meticulously planned to display the couple's art collection, including pieces by Abraham Palatnik, Alfredo Volpi, Candido Portinari, Damien Hirst, and Frans Krajcberg. Specially designed niches ensure that each work is framed and duly celebrated within the space.

CALATRAVA
Brazil
CHIC STAYS
MIAMI BEACH
PALM BEACH

VC Beach House

Angra dos Reis, Brazil
Area: 660 sqm (7,100 square feet)
Photography: Romulo Fialdini

When Italian explorer Amerigo Vespucci first arrived in Angra dos Reis in 1502, he famously wrote, "If there is a terrestrial paradise in the world, it cannot be far from this region." Such a sentiment perfectly captures the essence of this house, set on a private pier along the Costa Verde. Renovated while preserving its original structural pillars and beams, the home feels at one with its surroundings. "The deck almost embraces the sea, along with the pool, terrace, and gourmet kitchen area, offering access to a private beach," explains Guilherme Castello Branco. The architecture blends harmoniously with nature through expansive glass panes and wooden brise soleils that optimize cross-ventilation and natural lighting. The landscaping by Rodrigo Oliveira enhances the seamless dialogue between the house and the surrounding natural beauty.

les
américains

Toca Farmhouse

São Paulo, Brazil
Area: 1,890 sqm (20,350 square feet)
Photography: Tuca Reinés

The reflection of the architectural volumes on the lake's surface sets the tone for this expansive farmhouse. With thirty-two bedrooms, the house could easily feel more like a hotel, yet it retains the intimacy and warmth of a private residence. "The program had very specific requirements because the owners entertain frequently. The dining and breakfast rooms can host up to forty guests," says Guilherme Castello Branco. Designed for a large, traditional family passionate about sports, the property includes a swimming pool, gym, and sports courts. For gatherings, a barbecue area and pizza oven were built in a separate volume. Rodrigo Oliveira's landscaping completes the setting, framing the pavilions and anchoring the home in its stunning natural surroundings. One of the most striking features is the family museum pavilion, a space filled with photographs, artifacts, and the rich history of the owners.

Toca Farmhouse

Horizon

Toca Farmhouse

RD Residence

Campinas, Brazil
Area: 1,480 sqm (15,930 square feet)
Photography: Ruy Teixeira

The client, a mother of two children, requested a single-story house with the strongest possible connection to the garden. “We designed an H-shaped layout where much of the structure embraces the green spaces and the pool, both sculpturally designed by Alex Hanazaki,” explains Guilherme Castello Branco. Located in Campinas, São Paulo, this home combines coziness and sophistication while prioritizing functionality. On one side, the bedrooms enjoy privacy, while the other side houses the living room, dining room, gourmet kitchen, and terraces. “We concentrated the social and family spaces toward the outdoor areas, positioning the service zones discreetly at the rear,” the architect adds. The result is a family-friendly retreat that balances elegant design with relaxed living.

LOC Country House

São Paulo, Brazil
Area: 1,100 sqm (11,840 square feet)
Photography: Marco Antonio

The whimsical vision of a barn-style house in the Brazilian countryside was brought to life with precision in this sloped terrain near a lake. Unlike the colonial-style farmhouses commonly seen in Brazil, this project draws inspiration from contemporary industrial aesthetics. "When the client expressed a desire to feel as though they were on a deck, we immediately proposed elevating the house, creating a stone skirt to keep it above the damp soil. The two main levels then unfold above, with the upper volume clad in stone," explains Guilherme Castello Branco. The roof, made of black automotive-painted metal, reinforces the home's neo-industrial mood. Gilberto Elkis's landscape mirrors this subtlety, blending seamlessly with the natural setting. An additional spa and gym pavilion, overlooking the lake and pool, completes the program.

Interiors Atelier AM
CHIC STAYS
BOSPHORUS PRIVATE
NEW YORK
Modern Art
RITZ
WONDERS OF THE WORLD
Matisse Cut-outs

Spaces reflect culture. Dado's art placements open windows onto the world, inspiring beauty, ideas, and endless perspectives.

Art

If the spaces we inhabit are reflections of our culture, then our relationship with art becomes ever more significant. With thoughtful curation and an attuned sensibility, supported by collections large and small—each wall a repository of memories—the Dado Castello Branco architecture studio assembles and places artworks within the spaces as new windows toward the world. These works add beauty, provoke thought, and offer direction, shaping not only the physical environment but also the infinite possibilities that reside in the gaze of those who observe.

SoHo Apartment

Lower Manhattan, New York, USA
Area: 240 sqm (2,580 square feet)
Photography: Douglas Friedman

"This is a new building in the heart of SoHo, a neighborhood in New York dominated by prewar structures—classic brick buildings, often adorned with graffiti," explains Dado Castello Branco. The apartment, still in its planning stage when the project was commissioned, features contemporary solutions that perfectly capture the area's unique atmosphere. Floor-to-ceiling windows frame views of the surrounding neighborhood, blending the indoors with the lively urban setting. Brazilian design icons, such as Jorge Zalszupin's tea cart and armchairs, were carefully brought into the mix, alongside the 1958 *Ring Chair* by Nanna Ditzel. Art takes pride of place on the walls, with standout works by Hélio Oiticica and Beatriz Milhazes, two giants of Brazilian contemporary art with global resonance.

SoHo Apartment

COMPORTA
MYKONOS MUSE
DONALD
MICHELE BÖNAN
PRIVATE
ESCAPES
LIVING ON WATER

CHIC STAYS
NEW YORK

PICASSO

RDP Apartment

São Paulo, Brazil
Area: 293 sqm (3,150 square feet)
Photography: Marco Antonio

Highlighting an art collection—both for the enjoyment of its owner and for the admiration of guests—requires extraordinary expertise that goes beyond aesthetics. In this apartment, filled with works by renowned masters such as Sergio Camargo, Richard Serra, Anish Kapoor, Damien Hirst, and Zaha Hadid, the renovation was carefully designed to complement the existing collection while accommodating future acquisitions. "Although fluidity and integration are hallmarks of our studio, here we maximized wall space to properly showcase the art," explains Dado Castello Branco. Indeed, features such as a retractable screen in the home theater were introduced to avoid wasting wall surfaces. A window was closed and the custom lighting was meticulously planned to illuminate each piece without creating shadows. Even the powder room features a stretch ceiling for diffused, unobtrusive lighting that enhances the collection.

les must de Cartier

Cinthia Marcelle
AMELIA TOLEDO

COMPLICADO
WIND
MATER

VAI VER SE ESTOU

Ibirapuera Apartment

São Paulo, Brazil
Area: 591 sqm (6,360 square feet)
Photography: Marco Antonio

The role of the architect transcends form and function: it is about creating spaces that inspire connection, foster daily routines, and ignite meaningful experiences. "In this apartment, which we virtually stripped to its bones and rebuilt, the idea was to accommodate the family dynamic," explains Dado Castello Branco. Designed for a father with four children, the layout includes a home office adjacent to a family room, ensuring proximity to the kids. A large terrace dining table fosters collective meals, whether in daily life or for special gatherings. Additional features include a wine cellar and a striking dining room framed by a custom portico. Upon stepping out of the elevator, the panoramic view of the owner's impressive art collection sets the tone for the home—an elegant intersection of personal narrative and contemporary living.

VISIONAIRE
DALI

LOC Apartment

Manhattan, New York, USA
Area: 192 sqm (2,070 square feet)
Photography: Fran Parente

"With limited windows, we wanted to create a sense of landscape within the living area, which we achieved through a hyper-realistic artwork depicting nature that visually oxygenates the space," says Guilherme Castello Branco. This New York apartment perfectly reflects the studio's signature, that is, Brazilian DNA with a cosmopolitan identity. The interiors are marked by low-profile sofas, curated antique finds, and a selection of contemporary design pieces. The highlight is a Pop Art painting by American artist Alex Katz, which lends energy and character to the living space. "In this project, the view isn't essential—the carefully chosen pieces bring the space to life in an equally impactful way," adds the architect.

THE TREE Meaning and Myth
MORNING NOON NIGHT
Andy Warhol—From A to B and Back Again

Naples and the Amalfi Coast
TARSILA DO AMARAL

GISELE
PLANT

Glenfiddich
ACQUA PANNA
TOSCANA
NEW YORK COCKTAILS
COFFEE

Belgravia Apartment

London, UK
Area: 135 sqm (1,450 square feet)
Photography: Ben Anders

Located in an eighteenth-century building in London's exclusive Belgravia neighborhood, this apartment underwent a full transformation to meet contemporary needs while preserving its historical essence. "The project was about updating a space that the family has owned for over forty years, modernizing it without compromising its character," says Dado Castello Branco. The addition of air-conditioning—now essential for increasingly harsh European summers—was one of the key updates, along with the removal of an obsolete fireplace. "We replaced the fireplace with an extended living area, featuring a B&B Italia sofa and a standout work by Vik Muniz, which creates a striking dialogue with the family's collection of Johann Moritz Rugendas prints," he notes. The previously compartmentalized layout was ingeniously reimagined: hallways were removed and sliding doors replaced fixed walls to improve flow and connectivity. The library was transformed into a functional home office with a sofa bed for guests. Located near Harrods, Buckingham Palace, and Hyde Park, the apartment perfectly balances tradition and modernity.

Belgravia Apartment

Entertaining Chic

Garden Ornament

GREAT ESCAPES ITALY
HOTEL DU CAP EDEN-ROC
PALMS

EA Apartment

São Paulo, Brazil
Area: 528 sqm (5,680 square feet)
Photography: Fran Parente

The transformation of this originally dark and overly compartmentalized São Paulo apartment focused on enhancing natural light and spatial flow. The layout was redefined with strategic interventions to create openness and harmony: "We prioritized the connection to the exterior and created visual permeability by integrating the living areas," explains Guilherme Castello Branco. The design highlights refined wood paneling and seamless cabinetry running from floor to ceiling, contributing both to aesthetics and functionality. Furnished with a mix of Brazilian modernist classics and contemporary international pieces, the interiors exude understated sophistication. The carefully curated art collection adds personality and color, punctuating the neutral palette. "The result is a space that feels elegant, practical, and deeply attuned to the clients' lifestyle," concludes the architect.

Monet

Riva
GÊNESIS

BASQUIAT

Biographies

Dado Castello Branco

A leading name in Brazilian architecture with an international footprint, Dado Castello Branco has built a career spanning over three decades, defined by elegance and meticulous craftsmanship. His work has made its mark across the Americas and Europe, blending Brazilian modernist influences with a refined take on classical design.
A graduate in Architecture and Urbanism from Faculdade Belas Artes de São Paulo, he furthered his studies at the École Spéciale d'Architecture in Paris. His signature approach combines perspective, seamless indoor-outdoor integration, bespoke furniture design, and a meticulous curation of fine arts, resulting in cosmopolitan projects with striking aesthetic and ergonomic depth.

Guilherme Castello Branco

The eldest son of Dado Castello Branco, Guilherme has not only followed in his father's footsteps but is also the director of the namesake firm, where he has been shaping projects for nearly a decade. Recognized as one of Forbes Under 30's rising talents in 2024, he is an architect and product designer trained at Fundação Belas Artes de São Paulo. With a sharp eye and a broad expertise spanning residential and corporate projects, he has also been channeling his creativity into object design. In 2025, he is set to launch his own furniture brand, Jequitibá.

Ricardo van Steen

Born in 1958, Steen lives and works in São Paulo. He studied art, cinema, and design, and has practiced the three activities simultaneously since 1980. His work is based on the displacement of concepts between graphic design, art, and cinema, resulting in films, paintings, photographs, books, brands, and pieces of furniture.

As a designer, he planned and oversaw more than twenty titles—among newspapers, magazines, and television channels. He designed and published books for renowned architects in Brazil and signed the catalog for one of the São Paulo Architecture Biennials. As an artist, he is represented by Ralph Camargo Galeria; he has had five solo exhibitions and has taken part in several group shows in museums and galleries in Brazil.

Allex Colontonio

He is a journalist, creative director, and design critic. He has led major publications such as *Casa Vogue*, chaired the cultural department of the Latin America Memorial Foundation, and is currently the director of magazines *Pop-se* and *Forbes Design*. He wrote the text for this book.

This book would not have been possible without the support and dedication of the following:

AD.STUDIO por Paloma Danemberg

Arnaldo Danemberg Collection

Augusto Moreno Closets

Brada Mármores

Casual Móveis

Casulo Design

Celina Dias | Tecidos e Papéis de Parede

dpot

Entreposto

Etel Design

Fairbanks & Pilnik Construções Especializadas

Florense

Móveis e Decorações Russo

Otavio Castello Branco

Phenicia Concept

Troianos Automação

Vitrine

+55design

pp. 37, 38–39, 42–43: *Colour Splat*
© Ian Davenport by SIAE 2025

p. 55: *The Crucifixion*
© Vik Muniz by SIAE 2025

p. 78: *Alchimie 370*
© Julio Le Parc by SIAE 2025

p. 95: *Rio de Janeiro Postcard*
© Vik Muniz by SIAE 2025

p. 113: *FW Voiceless and Silent*, 2022
© Philippe Decrauzat by SIAE 2025

pp. 143, 146: *Ten Hummingbirds*
© Vik Muniz by SIAE 2025

p. 165: *Psalm - Exaudi, Domine*
© Damien Hirst and Science Ltd.
All rights reserved

pp. 229, 231: *Untitled*, 2012
© Anish Kapoor. All Rights Reserved,
DACS/ SIAE

p. 235: *Chloropropane*, 2006
© Damien Hirst and Science Ltd.
All rights reserved

p. 245: *Hummingbirds*
© Vik Muniz by SIAE 2025

pp. 251, 253: *Grey Dress M*
© Alex Katz by SIAE 2025

pp. 259, 266–267: *View of Rio de Janeiro*
© Vik Muniz by SIAE 2025

pp. 269, 274, 278–279: *Alchimie 335*
© Julio Le Parc by SIAE 2025

All images in the book were created with the permission of the homeowners at the time of the photo shoot. Every effort has been made in good faith to trace the copyright holders and obtain permission to reproduce the artworks that appear in the spaces in this book. The Publisher may be contacted by entitled parties for any iconographic sources that have not been identified.

FSC
www.fsc.org
MIX
Paper | Supporting responsible forestry
FSC® C084761

Art Direction and Graphic Design
studio olga

Distributed in English throughout the World by
Rizzoli International Publications, Inc.
49 West 27th Street
New York, NY 10001
www.rizzoliusa.com

ISBN: 978-88-918428-1-7

Printed in Italy
2025 2026 2027 2028 / 10 9 8 7 6 5 4 3 2 1

The authorized representative in the EU
for safety and compliance is
Mondadori Libri S.p.A., via Gian Battista Vico 42,
Milan, Italy, 20123
http://www.mondadori.it

Visit us online:
Instagram.com/RizzoliBooks
Facebook.com/RizzoliNewYork
X: @Rizzoli_Books
Youtube.com/user/RizzoliNY